Poetry for God

JEAN MARIE PATTY

PROMINENT
BOOKS

5830 E 2nd St, Ste 7000 #9983
Casper, WY 82609
USA

CONTENTS

BIOGRAPHY

Jean Marie Patty was raised in Anniston, AL. She has also lived in
California, Florida, New Hampshire and Atlanta.

She studied at Florida State University and loved writing and
art courses.
She also loves photography.
She loves God, family, friends and her cats.
Jean Marie hopes that all who read her book will find inspiration.

FORWARD

First of all, I would like to say that I wrote this book because of my
unfailing love for my King and Savior, Jesus Christ!
He has provided me with so much happiness and autonomy!
Without Jesus, I would have never been able to have found the
words for these poems!
Thank You, God, for all your blessings and gifts!
You are so amazing and wonderful, and I love you with my
whole heart!
I'm also thankful that you gifted me with my two precious kitties,
Cream Puff and Evangeline! They do make my life complete!
Without your love, Lord, I am nothing!
I sincerely hope that anyone who reads this book will find true
inspiration as my book was inspired by God!

ACKNOWLEDGMENTS

I would like to dedicate this book to my loving sister and best friend, Joan, and my other best friend, Janee!
My sister took care of me, for five months, while I was very sick.
She is so amazing! I love her dearly! She means everything to me!
My sister is a very warm person and a wonderful caregiver!
I met my friend, Janee, because of my illness. I am so thankful that we became so close! She helped me see life in a whole new light because of her positive outlook! She is awesome!
I give all the glory to God above for giving me all the words for my poems!
You are the greatest gift I have ever known!
God helped heal me from a very difficult illness. I love Him with all my heart and soul. I will always love Him, no matter what obstacles I may face!
I would like to thank my brother, Jim, for always being very supportive of my writing career. He is very special to me!
I want to thank my friend, Karen, for always supporting me in my artistic endeavors!
You are incredible and Your love for Jesus inspires me so much!
A very warm thanks goes to my friend, Donna, and her children, Aleah and Christian!
They are all so wonderful and I love them very much!
A very special thanks to Nancie, Kelli, Rosemary, Jennifer, Judith, Ann, Kathryn, Vickie, Debbie, Susan, Brandy and Ann-Marie!
You are all so supportive and wonderful to me!
Thanks to all my other friends who love Jesus!

Last, but certainly not least, a very special thanks goes to
my publisher,
Prominent Books and Natalie Clarke and Alesia Crae!
You have helped me bring my dreams to reality!

Amazing Grace

Gracie is sweet
and she is funny too.
She does my heart good
and that is so true.

Gracie loves my babies
and that means everything.
She is so precious and
she makes my heart sing.

Jean Marie Patty

Autonomy

God changed my life drastically
and gave me autonomy.
He is our Creator and
He is everything to me.

Jean Marie Patty

Beautiful Joan

My sister is so sweet and
I just love her so.
She is everything to me and
I cannot let her go.

My sister takes care of me
and helps me feel alright.
She's beautiful inside and out.
She is never far from sight.

Joan helps me to heal and
she is so special to me.
Joan is a wonderful person.
She lets me feel so free.

Joan is so funny and
cute as she can be.
She always makes me laugh
and fills my heart with glee.

Jean Marie Patty

Friends

I love Ann
and Willie Mae.
They are sweet
and make my day.

Ann and Willie are nice
and they are so kind.
I just adore them and
they blow my mind.

Jean Marie Patty

Give God The Glory

I give all the glory
to God up above.
He is awesome an
is filled with great love.

He helps me to write
and lets me create art.
He is so wonderful
from the very start.

Jean Marie Patty

Glorious Jesus

I want to be with Jesus
for all eternity.
For He is glorious
and gives me serenity.

Jean Marie Patty

God Is Always Good

The Lord has always
done great things.
He is awesome and
makes my heart sing.

I love the Lord
with all of my heart.
He is always good
right from the start.

Jean Marie Patty

God Is Gracious

I know God loves me;
I try to be nice.
He loves His children;
He doesn't think twice.

God loves everyone
even when we're wrong.
He always forgives and
we praise Him in song.

God is gracious
and loving and kind.
He is so sweet and
He's always on my mind.

Jean Marie Patty

God Is Precious

Lord, You are kind and
You never fail me.
You are so precious,
but I am not worthy.

You answer my prayers
and You never leave.
You are extremely awesome
and I truly do believe.

Jean Marie Patty

God Loves Me

The stupid enemy
tries to get to me,
but God is healing
and sets me free.

God helps me to see
that all will be okay,
and He will love me
forever in a day.

Jean Marie Patty

Gortie And Vangie

The babies love me
and I feel sublime.
They are precious
and they're all mine.

Jean Marie Patty

He Always Knows

Jesus is so kind;
He helps me through.
He always knows
just what to do.

I love You God
for You are Holy.
I am always Yours
and You are the Only.

You are the Only One
who can help me see
that it will be alright
and You will never leave.

Jean Marie Patty

He Is Everything To Me

God will always
carry me through,
because He is kind
and awesome and true.

I love my sweet Lord
so very much.
He is precious and
has a loving touch.

I will never leave Him,
for He is my King.
He is so wonderful and
He is everything.

Jean Marie Patty

He Is First In My life

Jesus, You are everything to me.
That's the way it'll always be.

Because I love You so much,
You have a sweet and precious touch.

You make me feel fine.
You will always be mine.

Jesus, You keep me from grief.
In You, I always find relief.

Jesus, You keep me from strife.
You are always first in my life.

I love You forever!

Jean Marie Patty

He Is Grace

I love my Lord
for He is good.
I love my Lord and
I do what I should.

For I love Him and
He is my saving grace.
He is merciful and
He knows my name.

He is perfect and
He makes me smile.
Will You please stay,
if only for awhile.

Jean Marie Patty

He Is Great

Lord, please help me
as I am afraid.
I need Your guidance and
all that you've made.

Your glory and goodness
are just what I need.
I love You forever and
You are great indeed.

Jean Marie Patty

He Is Kind

I need the Lord
in my life.
He always keeps me
far from strife.

When I'm feeling down,
I ask Him for relief.
He always listens
and cares beyond belief.

For the Lord is good
and knows my name.
He is forever kind
and remains the same.

Jean Marie Patty

He Is My Sword

I will never be ashamed
of my love for the Lord.
He is kind to me
and He holds the sword.

The sword is His strength
and he gives it to me.
He helps me with strife
and He will set me free.

Jean Marie Patty

He Is Wonderful

My Lord my King
is awesome and proud.
I always choose to sing
His praises out loud.

Jesus is merciful
and loving too.
He is wonderful and
my love for Him is true.

Jean Marie Patty

He Reigns Above

I love my precious God
with all of my heart.
He has been amazing
right from the start.

I cannot live without
God's everlasting love.
He is the Almighty and
He reigns from above .

Jean Marie Patty

His Gracious Blessings

Thank You Jesus
for allowing me to do
what I love and
love what I do!

You are the most amazing
God and I love You
so immensely!

Thank You for giving
me the words for my poems!

I love You forever!

You are the Most High and
You never leave my side!

Jean Marie Patty

His Kind Ways

I choose to pray
all of the time,
because I know that
He is all mine.

He gets me through
the toughest of days.
I love my Lord and
all of His kind ways.

Jean Marie Patty

I Love God

God is kind and
merciful and true.
He healed me when
I didn't know what to do.

He is mighty, awesome
and proud.
I love Him so much.
I sing His praises out loud.

Jean Marie Patty

I Love Him Completely

I love to rhyme
all of the time.
God is awesome
and He is mine.

Jesus is the reason
for all that we do.
I love Him completely;
He always sees me through.

Jean Marie Patty

I Love My Sister

My sister is kind
and often misunderstood.
She's got a heart of gold
and she tries to do good.

I love my sister
so very much.
She's my best friend and
we love to talk and such.

Jean Marie Patty

I Need Jesus

Jesus, I want You so and
You are so very true.
You have blessed me
and I love You.

You are generous
and so very kind.
You are in my heart
and always on my mind.

You are everything to me.
I'll never let You go.
I need You so much
and that is what I know.

Jean Marie Patty

I Place My Heart With God

It's a new day
and a fresh start.
Where do you want
to place your heart?

We should place it in
the loving faith of God.
Yes, He is awesome and it's
really not that odd.

Jean Marie Patty

I Sing Your Praises

I praise Your Holy Name, Lord
for you are everything.
With You in my life,
I want to dance and sing.

I sing Your praises
for You are good.
You are mighty and
I'm always understood.

You know my name and
You help me with my pain.
You are merciful and
You keep me sane.

Jean Marie Patty

I Will Be Alright

The trials were horrible and
I didn't know what to do,
but my love for Him endured
and this much is true.

I thought I would die,
but it wasn't my time.
He helped me go on and
then I was just fine.

I'm not completely healed and
I've got a long way to go.
But God is so loving
and He always lets it show.

Jean Marie Patty

Janee Is Sweet

Lord, let my friendship
with Janee grow and grow!
I love her so much
and cannot let her go!

Janee is so sweet
and so very neat!
She is really funny
and that you can believe!

Jean Marie Patty

Jesus Is Faithful

I know this to be true;
I do truly love You.
You are my everything and
You make me want to sing.

Jesus will never change;
He always stays the same.
He is so powerful and
He knows my name.

My sweet, precious Lord
is always so faithful.
He is kind and
so very beautiful.

Jean Marie Patty

Jesus Is Good

I love Jesus
because He is good.
He is awesome
and I'm always understood.

Jean Marie Patty

Jesus Is Sweet

I love You Jesus
until the end.
You have always been
my sweet, precious friend.

For You are everything
and You make me smile.
I can't do without You
even for a while.

Jean Marie Patty

Jesus Is Victorious

I know this to be true;
this is my reality.
You are my whole life and
You provide tranquility.

You give me sweet love
all of the time.
I am Yours always
and You are all mine.

Stay with me forever
and never leave my side.
You are everything to me;
from You, I cannot hide.

I can't hide from Your love,
for You are glorious.
I will always love You
and You remain victorious.

Jean Marie Patty

Jesus Loves My Babies

I love Puff and Vangie
so incredibly much.
They are beautiful and
soft to the touch.

God gave them to me
to have and to hold.
He is wonderful and
I am forever sold.

I'm sold on His love as
He has blessed me.
I love my sweet Jesus;
He is the Almighty.

Jean Marie Patty

Jesus Understands

I have to be discerning
as I am always yearning
to do my very best.
He puts me to the test.

I try hard for Jesus
and He always understands.
For I am not perfect,
but He always holds my hands.

Jean Marie Patty

Life Is Difficult

It's a vicious cycle
that leads to despair,
but look to the Lord
as He will be there.

Never give up hope
for God is so good.
Life can be difficult
but we are always understood.

Jean Marie Patty

My Best Friend Is Jesus

I love my sweet Jesus
all of the time.
He is my Savior and
forever He is mine.

I love Him so much
until the end of time.
Jesus will always be
a true friend of mine.

Jean Marie Patty

My Dear Friend Nancie

Nancie is my dear friend.
She is so very kind.
I love her to pieces and
she just blows my mind.

Nancie is supportive of all
of my endeavors.
She is so smart and
is really quite clever.

Nancie means the world to me;
I just adore her so.
She is very loving and
she certainly seems to glow.

Nancie has a love for the Lord
that is so very inspiring.
She is just awesome
and so worth admiring.

Jean Marie Patty

My Friend Ann

Ann is a lovely person
and also she is kind.
She is very special
and is always on my mind.

Ann loves the Lord
and sings His song.
We talk of Jesus
and we share for so long.

I love sweet Ann
with all my heart.
She is my friend and
we're never far apart.

Jean Marie Patty

My Friend Janee

Janee and I met
because I was in pain.
We really hit it off
and there is more to gain.

We have a lot in common
and we love to share.
Janee is so precious
and I will always care.

God brought us together
so that we could truly see,
that everything will be alright
and we can be set free.

I truly adore Janee
because she is so kind.
To think of life without her
would simply blow my mind.

Jean Marie Patty

My Friend Kathryn

Kathryn is my good friend.
We go back a long way.
She is very kind and
she just makes my day.

Kat is very talented and
loves cats like I do.
She is something special
and that is so very true.

Jean Marie Patty

My Friend Kelli

Happy Birthday Kelli.
I love you so.
You are precious and
that is all I know.

You are a child of God.
Your faith encourages me.
You are my true friend.
You fill my heart with glee.

I have loved you
for such a long time.
You are so special and
a dear friend of mine.

Jean Marie Patty

My Love For Jesus

I love Jesus
every single day.
I love Him so much
in every way.

Jesus is truly
my very best friend.
I will love Him
until the very end.

For He is my Father
and I love Him so.
This much is true,
I'll never let Him go.

Jean Marie Patty

My New Life

I love my new life
and Jesus is awesome.
He is always near
and I can blossom.

Jean Marie Patty

My Precious Karen

Karen is my dear friend
and she is very kind.
I love her so much;
she is a wonderful find.

Karen helps me get better
when I am feeling sad.
She is always healing
and she never gets mad.

I adore my precious Karen.
She is so very sweet.
She is my special friend and
she is an awesome treat.

I need Karen in my life.
She is so very dear.
I always think of her and
she is always near.

Jean Marie Patty

My Sister, Joan

Joan is my best friend and
I love her to the end.
She is good to me and
helps set me free.

My sister is so very
sweet and kind.
She is a wonderful find and
is always on my mind.

Jean Marie Patty

My Very Best Friend

My sister and I have
such fun together.
We laugh and bond and
through any storm we weather.

We have spent our
lives just sharing.
We have always loved
and are forever caring.

My sister will always be
my very best friend,
and I will love her
to the very end.

I thank my Lord
in Heaven above
for my precious sister
that I truly love.

Jean Marie Patty

Our Lord Is Kind

I need Your love
through every single day.
I love You Lord and
forever I will pray.

You are merciful
and so very kind.
You are everything and
You're always on my mind.

I need Your grace
to see me through.
For You are mighty
and awesome and true.

Jean Marie Patty

Our Redeemer

My Jesus is perfect and
that is what I know.
He is our Redeemer and
I let my love for Him show.

Jesus answers my prayers
and He is always kind.
He always forgives and
He never leaves my mind.

Jean Marie Patty

Peace of Writing

Writing is quite often
a rather cathartic release.
I enjoy it so much;
it brings me such peace.

Jean Marie Patty

Precious Donna, Aleah and Christian

Donna is my friend and
I love her to the end.
She is so very kind and
she always blows my mind.

Donna teaches me to paint as
she is so very smart.
She means the world to me.
I loved her from the start.

I love Donna's children
because they are so sweet.
Aleah and Christian are wonderful.
They knock me off my feet.

Jean Marie Patty

Precious Janee

My sweet and loving Janee
always makes my day.
She is so precious
in every single way.

I think she is awesome
and so very kind.
She is a lot of fun
and simply blows my mind.

I hope that we become
the very best of friends,
because I'll always care
until the very end.

Jean Marie Patty

Puff & Evangeline

Cream Puff is fine
and she's all mine.
I love her so and
I'll never let her go.

Vangie is beautiful
and so very sweet.
She is just lovely and
is a special treat.

I love them both
much more than life .
They're both awesome
and never cause strife.

Jean Marie Patty

Stay With Me

I love You Jesus
so very much.
You are kind and true
with a sweet gentle touch.

You make me happy and
You make me smile.
I know You will always
stay for a long while.

Jean Marie Patty

Thank You Lord

I just love my
precious Janee!
Thank You Lord
for our visit today!

We had fun and
laughed and such!
How I love her
so very much!

Jean Marie Patty

The Joy of Writing

How I love to write
every single night.
It's a form of expression
that keeps me from suppression.

Jean Marie Patty

The Words Are Freeing

Writing is an outlet
that just sets me free.
I love it every day
and that you can believe.

God gives me the words
for He is all knowing.
I worship Him always
and He is just glowing.

Jean Marie Patty

You Are Faithful

Lord, please don't put
too much on me.
I get so afraid and
I also get lonely.

I know You hear me
when I call Your name.
You are so faithful and
You always keep me sane.

Jean Marie Patty

You Are The Greatest

Lord, I need You
every single day.
I love You so much
and I will always pray.

I am especially sad
about my sweet Puff,
but Your love is pure
and is always enough.

I love You so much
with all of my being.
You are the greatest and
You are always worth seeing.

Jean Marie Patty

SYNOPSIS

Jean Marie wrote this book during some very difficult trials.
She always relied on God for her healing.
Her book is about God first, then family, friends and her two cats.
She loves all these with her whole heart and soul.

www.ingramcontent.com/pod-product-compliance
Lightning Source LLC
Chambersburg PA
CBHW020921140626
46545CB00015B/1106